1

Please feed me

Genesis 25 v 30

One day Jacob had cooked himself a stew. Esau came in from the fields and was very hungry. He begged Jacob for some of the stew but Jacob would only give him some if Esau gave him his birthright. This would mean that Jacob, the younger son, would receive all the blessings and privileges that the oldest son should get. Esau was so hungry that he agreed, and Jacob gave him the stew. This showed how little Esau's birthright meant to him.

Make me savoury food and bring it to me

Genesis 27 v 4

When Isaac was very old, and knew he would soon die, he called Esau and asked him to bring him some meat so that he could receive his blessing from his father. Rebekah was listening, and wished her favourite son to be blessed instead. She told Jacob to get two goats from the flock and she prepared them how Isaac liked them.

The voice is Jacob's, but the hands are Esau's

Genesis 27 v 22

Jacob dressed in Esau's clothes and Rebekah put the skin of the goat over his hands and neck so that he would feel as hairy as Esau, for Jacob had smooth skin. Jacob took the food into Isaac, and although he was confused by the voice he thought he recognised the hands, and so gave Jacob the blessing meant for the eldest son. Jacob was blessed with good crops, the loyalty and respect of all nations, and control over all his brothers.

Esau hated Jacob because of the blessing Genesis 27v41

As Jacob left, Esau came in and asked to be blessed. Isaac told him that he had blessed another who claimed to be Esau. He was very upset, because the blessing would be true for Jacob, just as the Lord had declared while they were in their mother's womb – "the older would serve the younger". He was very angry because Jacob had taken away his birthright and blessing but he asked his father for a blessing too. Isaac told Esau that he would live by the sword and would serve his brother, but would one day break free of his brother's control. Esau hated Jacob because of his deceit.

Surely the Lord is in this place

Genesis 28 v 16

Esau was determined to kill Jacob once Isaac was dead, but Rebekah heard about it. She told Jacob to go to her brother Laban, in Haran, to escape Esau. Isaac blessed Jacob before he left and asked that he choose one of Laban's daughters to marry. Jacob set out and when he got tired he lay down and slept. He dreamt that he saw a ladder reaching to heaven and angels were climbing up and down it. God was standing at the top of it and promised to be with Jacob. Jacob awoke and was really aware of God's presence.

He said to them, "Do you know Laban?"

Genesis 29 v 5

Jacob swore that he would accept the Lord as his own true God and he travelled on. He came to the east and saw a large well with flocks around it and asked the men tending them if they knew Laban.

BOOK 6 JACOB

Jacob rolled the stone from the well's mouth

Genesis 29 v 10

The men said they did. Laban's daughter Rachel was coming towards the well and Jacob rolled the stone away from the well's mouth and watered his uncle's sheep.

Laban ran to meet him

Genesis 29 v 13

Jacob kissed Rachel and wept with joy at having found her. He told her he was Rebekah's son and she ran to find her father. When Laban heard about him he ran out to meet him and embraced Jacob as his own nephew.

Jacob served seven years for Rachel

Genesis 29 v 20

Jacob stayed with his uncle for a month, then Laban asked him what his wages should be for all the work he was doing. Laban had two daughters, the eldest was Leah and the younger Rachel. Rachel was more beautiful and Jacob loved her. He told Laban that he would serve him for seven years if he could marry Rachel at the end of that time. Laban preferred that she marry Jacob than any other man and so he agreed. Jacob worked seven years for Rachel, but because he loved her so much it passed like a few days.

Was it not for Rachel that I served you?

Genesis 29 v 25

At the end of the time a great feast was held and Jacob was married. The bride wore a veil, and it was only the following morning that Jacob discovered that Laban had married him to Leah instead. Laban gave his maid Zilpah to be Leah's maid. Jacob asked why he had been tricked. Laban explained that the younger daughter could not be married before the older one.

She called his name Joseph

Genesis 30 v 24

After a week Jacob was given Rachel as a second wife but he was made to work another seven years. Laban gave Rachel his maid Bilhah as a wedding gift. The Lord made Leah have lots of sons because she was unloved, but made Rachel barren because she was loved so much. Jacob had twelve sons in all, with his two wives and their two maids. Ten of those sons were to become part of the twelve tribes of Israel. Later, Rachel had two sons, Joseph and Benjamin, whom Jacob loved most, because she was his favourite wife.

Laban blessed them and returned to his place

Genesis 31 v 55

Jacob now wished to leave Laban but his uncle did not want him to go because the Lord had blessed him while Jacob had been there. Laban no longer liked him but Jacob knew that God was providing for him and he was not afraid. Rachel and Leah were happy to leave with their husband and they all ran away. Laban chased them but finally let them go with his blessing.

Esau ran to meet him

Genesis 33 v 4

Jacob prepared to meet Esau but was afraid that his older brother would still be angry with him and would attack him. He divided his company into two groups so that at least one might escape and took many gifts and offerings to give to Esau. That night he wrestled with a man till morning but was not beaten, and the man, who was God, blessed him, and named him "Israel". That day Esau came to meet him and they embraced in love, and not in anger.

An outline of the life of Jacob

Isaac and Rebekah had twin sons named Esau and Jacob. Esau was the oldest and Isaac's favourite, but Rebekah preferred the younger, Jacob.

Esau was a clever hunter, and on one occasion he came home from the field very hungry. Jacob had just made some food and it seemed very good to Esau. He asked his brother for some of the food and Jacob said he could have it if he was given his brother's birthright. Because he was very hungry Esau agreed, and this meant that after their father's death Jacob had the right to take control of a double portion of Isaac's possessions.

As Isaac became old his sight began to fail. He called for Esau and asked him to hunt for some venison and make him a stew, so that he could bless Esau after he had eaten. Rebekah heard this and was determined to steal the blessing for Jacob. She took some goat meat and prepared this for Isaac. She covered Jacob with goatskin and Esau's clothes, to deceive her husband. At first Isaac was unsure who the young man was, but became convinced that it was Esau and after eating he blessed him. This meant that Jacob now had the rights that should have been given to the older son.

When Esau returned, he and Isaac realised what had happened and Esau wanted revenge. Rebekah heard Esau's threat and sent Jacob to her brother Laban, so that he could choose a wife from his uncle's daughters. One night on his journey he had a strange dream in which he saw a ladder from earth to heaven, with angels ascending and descending. It was through this experience that Jacob was aware of God's presence.

Jacob continued on his journey and came to Haran, where his uncle lived. When at a well, he asked where Laban lived and was told that his daughter, Rachel, was coming to the well to water the sheep. When Jacob met Rachel he rolled the stone away from the mouth of the well. Jacob said who he was and met Laban who welcomed him warmly.

Jacob stayed with Laban, who wanted to pay his nephew for working for him, but Jacob offered to work for seven years for nothing if he could marry Rachel at the end of that time. Laban agreed to this and seven years later there was a wedding. The bride had her face covered and Jacob did not know until afterwards that it was Leah. The custom was that the eldest had to be married first but if Jacob would work another seven years he could have Rachel. Jacob agreed to this because he loved her. Leah had six sons with Jacob, but it was a long time before Rachel had any sons. Her first was called Joseph.

Eventually Jacob longed to return to Canaan. Laban was unhappy about this because he had prospered with Jacob around, but finally they parted happily.

Jacob was unsure how Esau would greet him so he informed his brother of his return. Esau wanted to meet his brother after so long apart. On the journey Jacob sent his family ahead and spent a night alone. During that night of prayer he wrestled with an angel until he was blessed, and then continued his journey. The next day he met Esau and was warmly greeted by him. Jacob then settled in the land of Canaan with his family.

30

BOOK 6 JACOB

THE STORY OF JOSEPH. Jacob, who was also known as "Israel", had many sons and they lived in the land of Canaan. Joseph was Jacob's favourite and he made him a coat to show that he was his best-loved son. This made Joseph's brothers very jealous and they hated him.

Find out more in Book 7